NOT ALL
KIDS
DO DRUGS

Lessons in Drug Prevention:
Handbook One
Proactive Parenting Techniques

By
Miles To Go
Kelly Townsend, M.S. & Jonathan Scott

Les –
A little light retirement
reading for you!
Jonathan

Not All Kids Do Drugs
Lessons in Drug Prevention: Handbook One
Proactive Parenting Techniques

Copyright © 2010 by Miles To Go, Kelly Townsend & Jonathan Scott

Ordering can be done at www.milestogodrugeducation.com
Kelly Townsend, M.S. & Jonathan Scott

This book was developed from the Parent Meeting Lecture created by Miles To Go for their Drug Abuse Prevention Lecture Series. Miles To Go is based in Southern California.

The information contained in this book is meant to provide the reader with information for drug abuse prevention purposes only. It is not a substitute for medical advice, diagnosis or treatment. A medical professional should be contacted immediately in cases of substance abuse and possible overdose.

While the authors have made every effort to provide accurate information and internet addresses at the time of publication, neither the publisher nor the authors assume any responsibility for errors or changes that occur after publication.

ISBN: 1453794115

Our Philosophy For This Book

Years ago, when we first considered writing this handbook, we decided that most people have little or no desire to curl up with a cup of cocoa and a drug abuse prevention book. We'll never be considered a "fun read," and we won't make the "Top 10 books to bring to the beach." We have compiled a selection of the most valuable information in a handbook format that we feel is user-friendly, accessible, and consumable in small blocks of time. This is the first in a series of handbooks that will provide anyone parenting or working with kids the tools needed to support their efforts to keep those kids safe in a world full of drugs.

This book is dedicated to all the parents who grudgingly came to our presentation and walked away saying, "That was the best presentation I ever went to."

Table of Contents

Part 1

Answering The Big Questions

"All kids are going to do drugs, so why don't we teach them how to use safely?"

We might as well start with this common parental assumption—all kids will eventually try drugs, especially alcohol. Since this is our starting point, it's also where we'll make our first stand:

NOT ALL KIDS DO DRUGS!!

We can't tell you how often a parent in one of our presentations announces that, "All kids are going to do drugs." Without fail, at least a couple of parents who stayed silent in the face of this all-knowing pronouncement approach us after the event ends and say, "I've never done a drug in my life," or, "I've never had a drink or smoked a cigarette. Does that mean I can't teach my kid about this subject?"

In our drug abuse prevention presentations for parents, we've always encouraged schools and parents to *support the nonusers*—because the users have the loudest voice and will drown out the voice of the nonusers. We are astonished that, despite all we know about the costs associated with teen drug use and adult drug abuse, large segments of our society still perceive users as the cool group. The party people are seen as popular and cool, and they reinforce this image with a language filled with terms nonusers might not understand. This special slang acts to bring the users together and exclude others. They also have an easy time finding like-minded others—they just go to a party, look around--and *voila*--instant peer group. The most vocal members of the party group, the ones that lord their drug knowledge over less exposed members of their class or school, are a special breed. We refer to them as drug bullies. Nonusers tend to be scattered among the chess players, the musicians, the athletes, the rock climbers, the actors. They don't know each other, and they have a lot of difficulty identifying each other. These nonusers need encouragement to continue their conscious choice, and we need to actively encourage healthy alternatives to drug use.

A major problem, though, is that a few of these drug bullies don't change when they reach adult age. The parent who stands up and says, "All kids are going to use," may well be nothing more than an adult drug bully. The parent that doesn't stand up and insist, "No, they aren't," is still being bullied and may still to this day feel uncool about their lack of drug experience. They have told us repeatedly that they don't feel they have enough knowledge to speak up about the subject because they are not part of the supposed "in-crowd." They are the parents who don't get invited to, or choose not to attend, the parties where binge drinking is happening. They also don't attend parties where marijuana is smoked and everyone pretends it's cool as long as their kids aren't around to see it.

We've been teaching drug abuse prevention education in schools for a long time, and one of the things we are sure of is that *not all kids do drugs*. We've had many students get in touch with us years after they saw our program to tell us they still haven't used drugs.

Many are now married and starting families and careers of their own, and they did it without falling prey to the silly notion that all kids are supposed to use drugs as a part of growing up.

Of course, it would be foolish for us to think that out of the 10,000 kids we teach each year not one would drink or get high—far from it. We have also heard from some of those who did choose to drink or use drugs. Several of them told us that they stopped before they got into serious trouble; several others went into rehab sooner than they normally would have because of their knowledge that help was available. Many had friends in trouble and were able to help them find their way out of a bad situation. Unfortunately, there are some students we are no longer able to hear from, but that we hear *of*—they are the ones that didn't make it out the other side of the decision to use. They are the ones who died.

Let's Look At A Few Common Variations Of The Original Question:

1. "All kids will eventually use, so why not let them do it in the safety of our home?"

First, it is impossible to monitor a group of kids who are drinking and using drugs in your home unless you are a trained drug specialist or an ER doctor with all the meds and tools you'll need in your bathroom medicine chest. If you think you will stop them from drinking and driving by taking away their car keys, we can tell you from experience that some of the kids are smarter than you are—they bring a second set of keys. If drunks want to drive, they will drive. Before you have your "safe" party, ask yourself these questions: "Can I tell the

3

difference between a drunken, passed out teenager and a teenager who is in a drug-induced or alcoholic coma?" "How do I know if that teenager has alcohol poisoning?" "Do I know the complete health and addiction history of these people and their families?" "Do I know what other drugs and medications they may have used tonight?" If you don't feel 100% confident about everything mentioned above, then you are not capable of taking care of a group of teen drug and alcohol users.

Actually, if you think about it, even if you are confident about all of the above, you are still not capable of taking care of a group of using teens—there are just too many variables to deal with effectively. With so many balls in the air at the same time, even a pro can miss something important.

A tragic story we heard while back east illustrates this point exactly. Some parents felt confident they could manage the mayhem associated with a teen drinking party, so they allowed the party to take place at their home. As expected, some of the teen attendees got really drunk, and a few even ended the evening getting sick all over themselves, *but hey, that's what it's all about, right*? Unfortunately, nobody thought to monitor the little sister of the teen host and the daughter of the parents allowing the party. She, in her effort to emulate the behaviors of the teens she so much wanted to be like, drank alcohol also. When she got drunk enough to feel ill, she went upstairs and lay down on her bed, where she proceeded to lapse into a coma.

We weren't able to follow this story to its conclusion, but it does beg the question: Are you confident that these parents would act in a timely and responsible fashion if *your* child was the one passed out and possibly lapsing into a coma? They would certainly

4

be aware that their participation in and sponsorship of illegal teen drinking would be frowned upon by the very authorities they would be calling. They may well fail to make the call in an effort to avoid the legal consequences that await them if they do. Their hesitancy may well cost your son or daughter their life.

2. "I lived through the 60's, 70's, or 80's. I drank and smoked myself under the table, and nothing ever happened to me. Why can't I take care of my child and teach them to use responsibly?"

If you are convinced you are a ninja parent and will not let your kid get hurt, you are kidding yourself. Are you certain that your kid's drugs are the same drugs you were using 20 years or more ago? A lot has changed since then—the types of drugs that are available; their strength and purity; the way they are taken or used—all this and more has changed since the days of your past use.

In the fall of 2009, a woman approached Jonathan at a parent presentation hosted by one of our schools. She described to him her feelings as she was on her way to her first exposure to our program. She said, "My husband and I were children of the sixties and seventies. We thought that, because of our experiences with drugs and alcohol, we were perfectly capable of dealing with any questions that might arise about drugs. Then I sat through your meeting. As soon as I got into the car after the presentation, I was on the cell phone to my husband, shouting, 'You've got to get to one of these meetings—we don't know sh__!' Since then," she continued, "I've encouraged every parent I know to come when they get the chance. There's just so much new stuff out there. I don't think a lot of people realize that."

We read about and study the subject of drugs regularly and extensively. Almost everyone we talk to is scheduled to the gills—they don't have hours and hours each day to educate themselves about drugs and drug issues. We do it because we love it. We do it because we have made it our job. It's also our job to educate parents and make available a capsule version of what we've learned. A parent presentation is a great place to start, but we also regularly (and shamelessly, it seems) recommend our website, milestogodrugeducation.com, as an excellent starting point.

But now, let's go back to the question. We would also like to ask, "How do you know nothing has physically happened to you as a result of your cigarette, drug and/or alcohol use?" Unless you've had brain scans, liver function tests and lung exams over the years, you have no clear picture of what kind of long term changes resulted from your drug use. Updated drug research has taught us that there are many long-term consequences of drug and alcohol use that in the sixties and seventies we didn't know existed. A lot of new evidence indicates that alcohol plays a role in many forms of cancer[i]—we didn't fully appreciate that a few decades ago. We also know more about permanent brain damage caused by cocaine use. Also, while almost everyone knows that tobacco is harmful and deadly, a lot of them aren't up to speed on the potential damage done by some of the other smoked drugs like marijuana, methamphetamine, and cocaine.[ii]

Do you want to explain to your children why you are dying prematurely because of party choices you made 40 years ago? We ask you that question because it's one we ask ourselves as we send our second-grader off to school. The thought of her being alone because of choices we made decades ago makes our hearts ache. We brought her into this world, and she has loved us without reservation—we don't want to miss the journey that lies ahead! Unfortunately, we may have lost any say we had in that a long time ago.

3. "What about the way they use alcohol in Europe? Don't they drink at an early age and have no problems with alcohol at all?"

We are always fascinated by this question. At first it seems so rational and logical, but further study reveals the misunderstanding and confusion a lot of people harbor about alcohol use in Europe. We want to first point out what most of you already know—Europe is not a country, it is a continent broken up into many countries, each with its different customs, beliefs, and social systems. Those who point to France as a model for safe alcohol use by young people are misinformed. A recent study showed that while teens in France will use alcohol moderately while in the presence of adults, they abuse it the instant adult supervision is removed or absent.[iii] Most people also aren't aware that French males are significantly more likely than other European males to die early,[iv] and that major contributors to this increased mortality are their extensive use of alcohol and tobacco. It's also important to note that France has an alcoholism rate that is equal to or slightly greater than that of the U.S.[v] It's hard to understand how all this constitutes what the questioners refer to as "no problems with alcohol." Maybe it's just that an alcoholic in a beret looks less devastated than one gone hatless.

Those who want to use Italy as their example have a slightly stronger argument. Italy has traditionally had a lower rate of alcoholism than ours,[vi] despite the fact they allow and encourage the use of alcoholic beverages by children. There are, however, a few things we must note. In Italy, use by young people is limited almost exclusively to wine that has been diluted with water. This watered wine is understood to be a *food product, not an intoxicant*. It is used to enhance the experience of other food products, not to get drunk. This wine is almost always used at the dinner table, in the presence of parents (and often grandparents, too) with the understanding that use is encouraged but drunkenness is abhorred. Italian society also has traditionally dictated that a drunken teen was not cool-- they were offensive. Unfortunately, anecdotal evidence seems to indicate that recently this lack of acceptance of teen intoxication has been muted as Italy becomes less isolated as a result of their membership in the European Union. We feel they will pay a price for this loss of identity if they allow it to lessen their disapproval of teen drunks.

Here's the kicker, though—*we don't live in an Italian society*. You may actually be able to reconstruct an Italian model of alcohol use at your own dinner table, but when your children venture out into U.S. teen society they will carry no societal protection or prohibition against drunkenness. They will find themselves deep in a climate of alcohol abuse and the associated risks that culture carries. Anatomically, our children are basically the same as any other kid from anywhere else on the planet, and although regular light drinking, as is found in Italy, shows no direct negative effect on the livers of those teens, heavy abusive drinking (the type typically exhibited by U.S. teens) is quite hard on a juvenile's liver.[vii] Also, the frontal lobes of the brain don't typically mature until a person is well into their 20's. These brain regions, where we house many of the functions for planning, memory, judgment, impulse control, and reason are the same regions of the brain that are quickly and profoundly affected by alcohol. Finally, we must note the overwhelming evidence that shows the link between early, regular alcohol use and spectacularly increased rates of alcoholism in adulthood.[viii]

So, can you teach kids to use safely? We think that by telling your kids they can use safely in your home you are teaching them that the risks cited above don't apply to your family—that you are somehow different from everyone else. You teach them to ignore science and biology. You teach them to not respect their brains and their developing bodies. You teach them that common sense and proactive thinking aren't as important as having fun and being the life of the party.

Here's what we think you should teach instead: You can teach young people how to drink safely by being a safe role model, by not drinking and driving, by not drinking to get drunk, and by not using alcohol as an exclusive way to relax at the end of a rough day. Show them how to have fun and relax without alcohol, and assure them alcohol will still be there for them when they are old enough to use it safely and moderately. *Your actions are more powerful than your words.*

"What are some issues you deal with as drug educators that parents might want to know about?"

The lack of treatment facilities for teens is shocking, but not as shocking as how expensive treatment is and how little of its cost is covered by insurance.[ix] We are always looking for good referrals so families and schools can help a young person in trouble with drugs. When it comes to addiction, treatment is always preferable to punishment.[x]

Even more frustrating, though, are the parents, faculty, and administrators who have called us about children or other family members in trouble. Of course, each of these people calls us with the best intentions in mind. All have someone they care deeply about. They are seeking advice and formulating plans of action. Our frustrations usually lie in the fact that virtually all of these people are overwhelmed by how much commitment is required on their part if this outreach is to succeed. Getting someone help is harder than it seems: Who is going to choose the treatment facility? Who will fill out the necessary paperwork? Who will arrange for and make the payments? Who will approach the young person in trouble? What happens if said young person resists these efforts? What happens if they do accept the offered treatment but fail in their attempt to get clean?

In the face of this overwhelming list of complications, even the most dedicated crusader can lose hope—it's just more trouble and effort than they ever imagined, so they put it on the back burner and hope the problem will go away by itself. We worry about the people who aren't getting the help they need, and wonder how many years will pass before they do get help.

Another issue, mostly faced by parents and family members, is the sense of embarrassment and failure they feel about their loved one's drug problems. Our society has come such a long way in its efforts to make people more comfortable discussing addiction in the family, but there is more than just a lingering reluctance on the part of a lot of parents to deal with this openly. The problem will not get better if we just ignore it. Throwing your hands in the air and declaring that you have no control over your family situation is not the solution either. It's important to remember that people die from drug and alcohol abuse and addiction. While we all hope it won't happen to us or our children, it sometimes does, and it often does so, at first, in the most subtle ways.

Many drug education programs have for years insisted they be allowed to work without teachers or other adults in the room. Most claimed that the students were more likely to "open up" if there were no adult representatives from the community present; that the discussions would be ruined if they could not be done in private. We feel exactly the opposite is true, and worry about what actually occurs in that privacy.

The only thing that happens in our classrooms is drug education. Whatever form the discussion takes, it is certainly not therapy or a twelve step meeting. The assumption that we need privacy indicates that something secret is going on. Even if the privacy did allow for open disclosure of behavior that would trouble an adult from the community, we don't want the burden of deciding which secrets to keep and which to disclose.

We think it a bit disingenuous to invite open discussion and then reveal those secrets to faculty and administration under the guise of caring, and yet that is what would be required of us if we were to find out something that represented a danger to a student or community member.

We also believe that school-based drug education programs will not solve the drug problem all by themselves— they are just one piece of the puzzle. When teachers sit in on our lectures, they experience the same class the students do. Because everyone is on the same page, ongoing discussions about drug issues can continue well after we've moved on. We think these discussions also dovetail well with the conversations that happen in the homes of parents who attend the parent section of our visit. We eagerly await feedback from teachers about how they use our new homework page on our website in their efforts to engage students in life skills discussions.

The other thing teachers add to the experience is basically just another set of adult ear. Kids are extremely selective listeners, but even when they can repeat verbatim what was said, they often interpret the meaning of what was said differently than what was intended. We think it's critical that teachers be able to clear up misunderstandings and gently correct mistakes when they arise. The last thing we need is more misinformation about drugs being passed off as fact because, "That's what the drug guy said." Also, if parents ever need clarification of what was discussed, the teacher will be perfectly able to do the job.

Another challenge, one we're sure we have in common with just about every teacher on the planet, is the amazing ability of students to selectively listen.

We're convinced that the vast majority of the misunderstandings that occur are attributable to simple listening problems or distractions that occur at the most inopportune moments, but sometimes kids just want to twist the tail of a parent or teacher.

An example of the latter occurred when one of our contacts, the school nurse, got a call from a parent who questioned the appropriateness of Kelly teaching drug education despite the fact that she was smoking marijuana as a part of the treatment she was undergoing for cancer. The nurse, a very good friend of ours, asked, "Kelly, is there something you want to tell me?" Further investigation revealed that all this misinformation was the product of one fifth grade boy's effort to start some drama. Kelly didn't have cancer, nor was she smoking medical marijuana for any reason—this young man just made it all up based on a few things he had heard during the medical marijuana discussion in the class. While trying to repair the damage done by this young man's tales, Kelly and the nurse found that this simple lie had caused quite a bit of upset among the rest of the class— half of them were really worried about Kelly, and the other half were freaked out that they were being taught by someone who was smoking marijuana.

Another example showed how unreasonable a person can be when they react in fear, even if that fear is inspired by a teenage son out for some laughs at his mom's expense. At an evening meeting a number of years ago, a woman homed in on Jonathan the minute she came through the door. She quite seriously demanded to know why her son would come home from drug education and tell her that it was OK to take cocaine to treat his ADHD. Of course, one minute of rational thought would have helped her understand that any drug educator who made that statement would quickly and permanently be out of work, but this mom wasn't thinking rationally—she was terrified that some stranger was putting her son in danger. If Jonathan had actually said what she thought he had, the danger to her son would have been real, but it wasn't—the whole thing was created by a bored kid who wanted to fire things up a little.

Another child did almost exactly the same thing, and as it turned out, for almost exactly the same reason. On the way home from school, this student told his mom that Jonathan said, "It's OK to do drugs as long as you don't get addicted." The mom immediately called the school and demanded to know what was going on. A couple of phone calls later, it was determined that the student knew for a fact that we never said anything of the sort—he was just heating up his mom.

Each of these anecdotes points to a common theme we see over and over again as drug educators— people are justifiably afraid of drugs and what those drugs can do to their loved ones. Unfortunately, scared people act irrationally, and irrational people are hard to stop once they get on a roll. The damage they do before they calm down may be hard to fix, and things they say may be hard to take back. As parents, we get how scary this stuff can be, but we think a lot of good can happen if we learn to move away from the fear of drugs and toward a healthy, knowledgeable respect for them. Maybe then we'll see a little less craziness and a little more reason when we respond to situations that involve drugs, even if those situations are merely the result of a practical joke gone awry.

Sometimes our more dedicated practical jokers find themselves in hot water over what started as a prank. More than once we have run across a student who decided it would be cool to bring something to school and pretend that they had drugs. One young man simply collected a bag of grass clippings and told his classmates he had marijuana. Another gathered up chalk dust in a baggie and claimed it was cocaine. More ominous, since a real drug was masqueraded as another more powerful one, was the time a student brought No-Doz (potent caffeine tablets) to school and declared them to be ecstasy.

In the first two cases, the students were unpleasantly surprised to find that they had run afoul of their respective schools' drug policies. Since there was no real drug involved, neither of these students was expelled, but both had the opportunity to ponder the consequences of their actions as they served their suspensions. In the last case, there existed real potential for disaster. Granted, there is only one documented case of caffeine overdose that resulted in death that we are aware of, but hospital and poison control center records across the country are full of reports documenting adverse reactions to caffeine tablets. Some of these patients were admitted to the ICU due to the severity of their symptoms. The student in the last example had unwittingly created a real danger, and was lucky to remain enrolled.

A final note we want to make about issues we face at work concerns those schools that lack clearly outlined policies about how they deal with drug and alcohol issues in their communities. We have learned that unless schools adequately delineate their policies and responses to situations that involve drugs and alcohol, they will find themselves reacting in knee-jerk fashion to each new calamity. It has been our experience that unplanned and unpracticed responses, or no response when one is required, have the potential to end in disaster.

One such case involved a parent who regularly showed up at carpool with the odor of alcohol on her breath. Nobody knew what to do, and there was no policy in place to guide them, so nothing was done to address the problem. Inaction remained the status quo until this parent was leaving the parking lot one day after picking up her kids in carpool. Perhaps a little drunker than normal, she turned too quickly and ended up striking a parking meter in front of the school. We're sure the embarrassment the kids felt as their mom was arrested for DUI in front of the whole school was real and quite distressing. We're sure the mom felt awful and embarrassed about it as well, after she sobered up. Perhaps the most shaken up, though, were all the faculty members and administrators who had let this go on for far too long. Their perceived powerlessness put a lot of people in danger. In the right drunk driving accident those kids, their mom, and any number of other innocent people might have died. That it didn't happen was pure luck.

Unfortunately, this same situation plays out in a lot of different school activities. Sometimes, parents who have had a few drinks arrive to pick up the kids at the school dance. Parents regularly drive away from school fundraising events where alcohol is commonly provided. We're positive that no school wants a parent to get a DUI, but we're also very aware that those schools know that checkbooks come out more easily and the checks written are bigger after those parents get a little drunk. Sometimes they get a lot drunk. There exists here a huge conflict of interest that concerned school communities are eager to address. If you want a complete list of policies we think schools should discuss and enact, please contact us, or refer to our upcoming handbook, "A Fly on the School Wall."

Parents don't just make mistakes regarding their own behavior—they make mistakes in the name of protecting their children. Most parents act very appropriately when their kids mess up. They realize the potential opportunity for their children to experience the consequences of their behavior and learn from their mistakes. Unfortunately, we've seen more than a few parents try to buy, fly, yell, bully, and sue their way out of their child's rule breaking. Some parents' behavior is simply shocking. One case involved a student dismissed and sent home early from a school trip for an egregious violation of school rules. The parent arranged for the child to be intercepted upon touchdown at a US airport and immediately re-board another international flight for a return trip to the same city the child had just left. The parent also arranged a room at the hotel right next to the one the rest of the students on the trip were staying in.

The problem is obvious to everyone but the parent and the child. When a kid breaks a rule and the parent does everything in their power to eliminate the consequences, what message does that send about how lives are lived? There is a fine line between protecting your child from harm and going so far that the opportunity to learn from mistakes is lost or intentionally erased.

Part 2

What Parents Need To Know

Every time we speak to parents at our parent education meetings, the very first point we want to establish is this—never underestimate your power! It's really easy for parents to feel less than powerful. It can sometimes seem that the only reason your children even exist is to make you doubt yourself. Lots of kids are more than eager to recite a list of their parents' inadequacies—you're too strict; you're not cool; you're an embarrassment; you just don't understand! You are the only one in the world who acts like this—other parents let their kids do this or try that. You're the only one with both feet stuck firmly in the mud.

Even if you retain nothing else from this entire booklet, we will consider it a win if you just remember this: you are, by far, the most important influence your children will ever have in their lives. They look to you for all the most important life lessons—values, morals, self-confidence, life skills. You are the last line of defense, the one who will always be standing with arms open, welcoming them in even if the rest of the world has shut them out completely. So many children we meet whose parents have failed to act like parents are bereft. If you won't parent your child, nobody else will.

You can't think it's the job of the school, either. Schools educate in the arena of academics. While most of the schools we work with provide adequate time to discuss the intellectual aspects of ethics, life skills, and character, it is the job of the parents to impart values into their children's lives. It is the most important job you will ever do.

There's just one problem—it's so hard to tell if you're doing a good job! One of the most critical mistakes we see parents make is to look to their children for validation of their parenting skills. It is not your children's job to validate you—their job is to make you feel like an idiot! Many years ago, a fellow educator put it perfectly when she said, "Your job is to be the wall; their job is to grind you into gravel." Unfortunately, being a good parent rarely feels rewarding in the short run. A quote in an article in a small Colorado Springs newspaper summed it up by reminding us, "You have to be willing to be uncomfortable. Parenting should be significantly uncomfortable for large periods of time. And if it's not, you're not doing it right."[xi]

The good news is that if you do your job, if you struggle to parent well for significant periods of time, you will eventually be rewarded. When? When your kids finally have kids of their own, of course! One of the saddest things in Jonathan's life is that his mom died just four months before our daughter was born. He never got the chance to tell his mom, "Oh! *Now* I get it! You did all that stuff because you *loved* me!"

Communication

When you do talk to your kids, it's a really good idea to do your best to communicate as effectively as possible. Don't waste time and energy *not* getting your message across. Check our recommended reading list at www.milestogodrugeducation.com for some excellent books on communication if you want some guidance from the professionals. In the meantime, practice the most basic communication skill—checking for understanding. When you talk with your children, be sure you understand them and they understand you. After you say something, ask them to repeat back to you what they heard. If they didn't really get your meaning, rephrase your point and try again. When you are all on the same page, your conversation can continue.

Do the same when they say something to you—repeat back to them what it is you heard. You will be really surprised, if you've never tried this before, at how often you misunderstand and are misunderstood. While this exercise can be frustrating and time-consuming at first, it is much less frustrating and wasteful than spending a lifetime operating on bad information.

Start With The Basics

Parents regularly approach us after our parent presentation to talk about specific issues they are dealing with. Often, it feels like what they would like most is an *answer*—what can they do so this thing will just be *fixed*? This is a classic good news/bad news situation. The bad news is, there is no answer—drug issues can't be fixed by doing any one thing. The good news is that there are very specific, time-tested things everyone *can* do that will improve the likelihood of a positive outcome. It's very important to be clear here: you can do all these things, all the time, for a really long time, and still have a bad outcome. That does not mean they are not worth doing. Parents who apply these principles consistently are rewarded with seriously lower rates of drug and alcohol use on the part of their children.[xii] We think the worst mistake you can make, though, is to try something once and then give up because it doesn't work the first time. You may need to adjust these ideas to fit your circumstances, but don't quit after one attempt!

Remember, nobody's perfect. We don't think many parents will be able to do all the things we suggest all the time. Choose your favorites and start with those. When you get really comfortable with those, try a few new ones. If you have a favorite tip or trick you have found to be really effective that you don't see here, send us an email and we'll include it so others may benefit from your wisdom. The important thing is to *try*. To not try is to not parent.

Three Things That Will Change Your Child's Life

We have a few suggestions that we consider to be the basics for proactive parents. They are:
1. Have an active role in your teenager's life.
2. Have a curfew.
3. Have a stated policy of non-use.

1. **Have An Active Role In Your Teenager's Life.**
   Yes, right when it seems your teens want you *out* of their lives, you have to be *in* them. Here are a few ideas about what an active role looks like:

   a. <u>Know what's happening at school.</u> We are not talking about micromanaging children's homework question by question, but we do want you to be aware of what's going on at school that's big. When is the midterm? When is the science fair? When is the play? The game? When something big happens, ask how it went. This lets your children know that you appreciate they are busy and you care about how they are doing.

b. <u>Know your child's friends.</u> It would be hard to overestimate how important friends are in your child's life. A great friend can change a life, but so can a bad one. If your child has a friend who exhibits behaviors you find troubling, you have to be vigilant about the relationship's effect on your child. A friend who uses drugs is a direct threat to your child, and must be treated as such. Unfortunately, dealing with a bad friend can be a lot like dealing with quicksand—the more you struggle, the deeper and faster you sink. It pays great dividends here to address the *behaviors* that bother you, not the friend as a person. Perceived attacks on a friend will often be read as attacks on your child, so addressing the behaviors can take some of the sting out of the discussion. This much is certain, though—direct evidence of a friend's drug use constitutes direct evidence of that friend's potential to cause your child harm.[xiii] That situation must be addressed directly.

c. <u>Understand, and help your child understand, peer pressure.</u>

"The main consequence of saying no to negative peer pressure is not just withstanding 'the heat of the moment,' as most adults think. Rather, it is coping with a sense of exclusion as others engage in the behavior and leave the adolescent increasingly alone. It is the loss of the shared experience. Further, the sense of exclusion

22

remains whenever the group later recounts what happened. This feeling of loneliness then becomes pervasive but carries an easy solution -- go along with the crowd." Michael Riera, Uncommon Sense for Parents With Teenagers

We have made it a formal policy in our classroom never to use the term "peer pressure" until after a student has used it. Peer pressure may be one of the more loaded and misunderstood concepts we deal with. Most adults we meet think there is some monstrous group of adolescents out there that is actively and aggressively trying to force their child to change and conform. Many young people we meet say they see the term peer pressure, when used by adults, as a two-pronged insult—your friends are out to hurt you; and you are bound, like some sort of brain-damaged sheep, to mimic any behavior you witness. This does not mean we don't see peer pressure as massively powerful, we just think it's much more subtle than most parents think.

As we see it, the most powerful peer pressure is not generated by the peer group, but is more a form of self-talk that constantly assesses situations with an eye toward the idea, "What can I do to make sure I will be accepted?" Most groups will not insist overtly that your child conform, rather they act or speak or dress a certain way, and accept outsiders only if they are willing to do the same. This pressure to conform is much more subtle than the commonly held notion, and yet is no less powerful.

Proactive parents can help their child develop resiliency in the face of peer pressure by reinforcing the idea that the child is a valuable person worthy of thinking and behaving as an individual. Children should be taught that any person who requires them to act a certain way in order to gain acceptance is not worthy of friendship. This effort should start as early as possible and continue throughout the teen years.

d. <u>Know your child's friend's parents.</u> No, you don't have to have intimate relationships with the parents of every casual acquaintance in your child's life, but if your son or daughter is going to spend any meaningful amount of time with other parents, you should know who they are. When your child is with those other parents, on some level these people will act as parents to your child, even if you have never spoken to them. Remember, other parents may not feel the same way you do about some very critical issues. We constantly deal with the issue of parents who feel it is better for kids to drink or use drugs at their house rather than have them do it out on the streets. (We will address this extensively in another section of this handbook.) To us, this is flat out irresponsible, and we can't support it in any way, but you have to be aware these people exist. If your child is in their presence, that child is automatically at risk.

e. <u>Know what media your child is being exposed to.</u> What music do your children listen to? What movies have they seen recently? What do they watch on TV? If you don't know the answers to these questions, you may not be doing all you can to keep your children safe. Media have rarely been shown to directly cause drug and alcohol use, but they can create a climate that encourages their use.[xiv] You could literally spend the rest of your life watching youtube videos of kids doing drugs. Continued viewing of these videos by your children is probably not the best use of their time, and it certainly isn't just an innocent way to while away the hours. It's also really important to know which movies and TV programs your children are watching. There is a direct association between the number of R-rated movies your young children or early teens have seen and the likelihood they will smoke, drink alcohol, or do drugs.[xv] The more often your children see smoking in movies, no matter the rating, the more likely they are to smoke.[xvi] By the way, these are not minor differences we're talking about here—the risks increase dramatically as the number of R-rated movies climbs.

f. <u>Communicate regularly with other adults who have a supervisory role in your child's life.</u> Think about it—your child's teachers may spend more time with your child during the week than you do. A teacher or counselor may also have information about the groups your child is hanging out with that you can't easily access any other way. If they see variations in behavior or activities that they find troubling, an ongoing relationship with you will make it easier for them to alert you to these important issues.

g. Eat dinner with your children as often as you can. The Center for Addiction and Substance Abuse (CASA) at Columbia University, in a study sponsored by Nickelodeon, showed that the most positive thing you can do is eat dinner with your children. Parents who have dinner with their children five nights each week have children who are 50% less likely to smoke, drink alcohol, or use drugs than do parents who have dinner with their children two nights per week.[xvii] We know—life is complicated, you're busy, but try to make a point of eating dinner with your family as often as you can.. You'll be doing great work if you do.

2. **Have A Curfew**.   We think it's really important here to define what we mean by curfew. A curfew is not necessarily a fixed point in the day, but more a time that adjusts in accordance with what's going on in your child's life that day. The most important things to consider when determining when a curfew should be are what activities will take place and what the approximate transition time is from one place to the next. If the movie ends at 9:20pm, everyone wants to stop for ice cream, and the total drive time between movie, Ben & Jerry's, and home is 30 minutes, it's not unreasonable to have a 10:45pm curfew.

    Having a curfew should not be viewed as you playing the role of time cop—it's about keeping your children in the presence of adult supervision as much as possible. If they aren't directly in the presence of adult supervision, they should be in transition from one supervised setting to another without a lot of free time. Why? Because young people, especially when they are in groups outside the presence of adult oversight, are much more likely to do something they wouldn't do if there were simply an adult standing there.[xviii]

Curfews should also include the proviso that if any variations from the planned itinerary occur then a phone call must be made to update you on the changes. Also, if a curfew is going to be missed for any reason, a phone call must let you know why. If changes aren't noted or a curfew is missed without explanation, there should be a pre-arranged series of escalating consequences. Notice we said the consequences for violating the curfew should be known to your children *before* any actual violation takes place. Clearly stated and understood consequences for undesirable behavior actually allow your children to consider the costs associated with decisions, and may potentially be used as a valid way for them to avoid participating in actions suggested by the group. (We'll talk more about this later.)

When we speak of consequences, we are not suggesting that when your kids break the rules you must immediately squish them like bugs. Punishment should never be out of context, overly harsh, or so disproportionate as to be unenforceable. Try to always be sure the punishment fits the crime. The worst thing you can do is fire your biggest gun at the first infraction. Really—what do you do after that?

Please note that curfews don't just apply to late at night. We've heard from lots of local police departments about what happens between 3pm and 6pm—the time of day when a lot of parents mistakenly *think* their children are supervised when they really aren't. Young people who hang around with other unsupervised teens are more likely to have difficulties with drug use, sexual activity, and other undesirable behaviors and emotional difficulties.[xix]

Finally, a lot of parents we meet aren't aware that their towns have curfews for unsupervised teens. The town we live in at the time of this writing has a curfew for all minors that extends from 10pm to 6am. Nobody under 18 can legally be in a public place or on the premises of any establishment without a parent or guardian present. If your town has a curfew, it may be a tool you can employ when explaining your curfew rules to your children.

3. **<u>Have A Stated Policy Of Non-Use</u>.** We have occasionally sent surveys home with our students. The students are supposed to interview their parents and fill in the answers themselves. We were surprised at some of the answers we got to the question, "Do you have a stated policy of non-use for the children in your family?" Frequently, the handwriting on the answer sheets changed for those particular answers—the adults had apparently taken the answer sheets from the children and started answering in their own handwriting. Often, the answers started with words to the effect, "It should GO WITHOUT SAYING that drug use is not allowed in this house!"

We want this to be clear: *If it goes without saying, it goes unsaid.* Children do not realize or understand what their parents want from them unless it is stated clearly and often. We always wonder aloud, "How many times do you have to tell your children to pick up their socks before they actually do it?" Why, then, do some parents think their children will automatically not drink, smoke, or do drugs if that expectation has not been clearly and frequently outlined? We can't overstate the power of parents who regularly voice the desire that their children refrain from drug and alcohol use—parents who do will reduce the chances their children will use by half.[xx]

Some parents think that rules and expectations of non-use will alienate their children. Actually, despite everything your children may say to the contrary, rules and expectations make them feel protected and loved. Parents who try to win the favor of their children by being the "cool parent" or the "pal" are completely missing the point, in our opinion. Years ago, Jonathan was having lunch with a group of juniors when one young man said of another, "His mom is really cool. She lets us drink beer and smoke weed with her." In an absolute deadpan, the other young man said, "I have plenty of friends. What I really wish I had was a real mom." Remember, if you don't parent your children, there is nobody else to fill that spot. You don't have to be mean and unfriendly, but you do have to be the adult. As your children grow into adulthood, the respect you earned by parenting them well will pay the dividend of a lifetime of friendship.

Parents regularly wait too long to have conversations with their kids about drugs. Many seem to think that their kids won't think about drugs if they just don't mention them—they hope the subject never comes up. Actually, the earlier you start the conversations about curfews, expectations and values, the more opportunities you will have to initiate conversation that is natural and in context. Numerous studies show that one of the major reasons teenagers cite for *not* using drugs is that they don't want to disappoint or embarrass their parents.[xxi] If you let your kids know exactly what you want, they may surprise you—they may do everything they can to meet your expectations!

If you start with these three simple things—have an active role in your child's life, set curfews, and have a stated expectation of non-use—you have laid down a foundation that will allow you to build success after success on top of it. If you don't, or if you have a laissez-faire attitude, then you will probably reap exactly what you sow. The Partnership for A Drug Free America said it beautifully when they penned, "Silence isn't golden. It's permission."

After you've started with the big three, you can move more fully into the rest of the tips we've learned over the years. What follows are techniques and how-to's you might need when certain challenges come up. Again, most people can't do all of them all the time, but keep them in mind and do your best. It's a very powerful list!

Look For Teachable Moments—
No Lectures Allowed!

A lecture is not a conversation. As an adult, your life experiences can certainly be useful to your adolescent, but unless you can find a way to effectively *communicate* that knowledge, you might as well be talking to a mirror. Effective communication requires that information be both presented *and* received. A lecture is nothing more than a broadcast. Most students we talk to assure us that a lecturing adult sounds much like the wah wah wah wah of Charlie Brown's teacher. How are we supposed to talk to our kids, then? First, conversations about drugs and alcohol are most effective if they are in context. As drug educators, we are constantly on the lookout for opportunities and settings that call for these discussions.

If your kids watch TV, make an effort to watch with them occasionally. We're pretty amazed at how much underage drinking on TV is depicted as normal. Watch movies with your children, and when you see drug and alcohol use (which you will) try to pay attention to the outcome of the use you see. Are there any consequences that result from the use? Is the use portrayed as cool? Ask your kids if they think that's how it works in the real world. When you see underage drinking, ask them if they know people who act that way, and if they think things in real people's lives usually work out the way they do for characters in a movie or on a TV show.

Listen to the music your children listen to. Are there drug and alcohol references? Why? Do they serve a valid point, or do they serve as a glorification of a drug lifestyle without consequence? Look for billboards that reference drugs and alcohol in any way, and discuss them with your children. Be mindful to resist the urge to issue proclamations about how bad drugs are; instead, try to remember you are having a discussion. You are trying to understand what your children think rather than trying to make them think just like you do.

With a little planning, you can actually create situations that allow you opportunities to talk to your kids about important issues. For years, we have recommended a website called teachwithmovies.org as a way to foster discussion. For a nominal fee ($11.99/year in early 2010) you can access over 300 insightful film reviews, many with accompanying study guides that will allow you to look way smarter than you may have in past efforts to talk to your kids.

Pay attention to anti-drug ads on TV. When you watch an anti-drug ad, ask your children if they understand what the ad is trying to say—some ads are so abstract even we don't understand their point! Ask your children if they think the ad addresses a real problem, or if it just comes off as preachy. If you don't watch a lot of TV, log on to adgallery.whitehousedrugpolicy.gov to view an extensive list of 30 second drug spots. Some we think are pretty good, others we think are pretty lame, but the important thing here is: what do your children think?

One last suggestion for a shared media opportunity—if your kids are old enough, watch a few episodes of the award-winning A&E show "Intervention." We have to warn you, you should watch a few episodes by yourself so you can decide whether you should share them with your children. These are really gritty, and there is an overwhelming sense of desperation, sadness and loss that pervades the first three-quarters of each episode. The good news is that almost all the subjects do ultimately go to rehab, but the bad news is the same as it always is with addicts—most of them will fail over time in their attempts to get clean. As you watch the show with your children, please notice how each of the people documented has a complete and utter lack of joy. What they are doing is not fun, and it certainly isn't partying. When you realize that over 60% of young people who *do* use drugs and alcohol cite as their reason for use a desire to "feel good and have fun,"[xxii] this show is very powerful in its ability to highlight how much the reality of what happens to drug users can differ from the perception of what young people think will happen.

Be mindful of time when you try to have drug discussions with your kids. We always tell parents to think of them as discussion drive-bys—get in, talk for a few minutes, then get out! Unless your children are showing signs of absolute engagement, talk with them for a few minutes, and then drop it; after anything more than a few minutes you run the risk of lecture infection.

Have A United Front

The classic nuclear family, while desirable, is not the only family structure we deal with. Whatever form your family takes, it's really important that the adults present a uniform message when discussing drug issues with their children. If all the adults in a child's life insist on presenting their particular spin on drugs and alcohol to that child, they run the risk of delivering a mixed message. Young people don't thrive in a system built on mixed messages—they need clarity, not confusion. We are *not* saying you have to agree with each other on all things drug-related, just that you should agree on what is to be said to your children at any given point in their lives.

Years ago, Kelly worked with a family suffering the consequences of mixed messages. The dad, a very successful medical professional, smoked marijuana in college, but all his accomplishments later in life had convinced him that his drug use had caused no measurable damage. The dad was of the opinion that occasional drug use was normal and pretty harmless. The mom, on the other hand, was terrified, because their son had listened to his dad's message and had started his own drug use. Unfortunately, the son's use was *different* from his dad's—it started at a much younger age, it was much more extensive, and the drugs he was using were more varied and much more potent that those of his dad's era. So, dad says it doesn't really matter, but mom is terrified and wants her son to stop. It's not very hard to understand how the son could migrate toward the dad's viewpoint.

Ultimately, the outcome was positive. After a few months of intense discussion, the dad came to realize how much trouble his son was really in, and eventually even the son realized how much his life was falling apart. Much to the relief of his mom, his very concerned sister, and his new on-board dad, he eventually stopped using. The most powerful factor contributing to his decision to stop using was, to us, the fact that the dad finally stopped validating his son's own drug use. If you and your significant other can only agree on one thing, you should consider this as a top contender—try to find a common ground when discussing drug and alcohol issues with your kids. Obviously, we think this common ground should include the notion that drug use by teenagers is unsafe and unhealthy.

Make A Family Mission Statement

Yes, you can do this, and no, it is not a lecture! A recent Google search for "family mission statement" yielded 15,700,000 results. This is not a brand new idea—families have long had specific sets of values they believe in and model their lives around, but the notion of creating a document that outlines those values is much more popular now than it was just a few decades ago. On our recommended reading list we have a number of books and workbooks that discuss how to develop a mission statement for your family, but they barely scratch the surface of what is available to help you. Your mission statement might be a very formal, classically corporate document that you frame and hang on the wall (not really recommended), or it can be a poem you feel accurately reflects the values you want your family to live by, or a picture, or just a few bullet points.

The form it takes is much less important than what the family mission statement accomplishes—it defines the values your family uses to live honorable lives. The really positive thing that happens when you identify and state your family values is that you provide your children with foundational values that travel with them wherever they go. If you don't delineate and state your family's values, your children are much more likely to adopt the values of whatever group they end up in. Remember, not all parents think like you do. If you and your children have agreed to a family value that says, "Alcohol is for people 21 and older," they are much less likely to accept a glass of wine offered by some other kid's parent in their home.

Your family mission statement also gives your children a tool with which they can deflect offers of drugs and alcohol. We don't expect that adolescents will comfortably say, "My family and I have agreed that alcohol is for adults," but they can use that part of the mission statement as the reason for saying, "No thanks, I'm good."

Please don't try to create your mission statement in one burst of effort. You may want to spend 10 minutes a week talking with your kids over dinner about what you all think should represent your family values. One mom recently shared her family's technique for developing a family values statement, and we loved it so much we want to share it with you. Her idea was to have a huge piece of poster-sized paper taped to the refrigerator door. At the top was the title, "How To Be A Smith." (Insert your family name in place of theirs, obviously.) Everyone in the family was welcome to write whatever they thought it meant to be a member of that family. To keep it light and truly focus it on her family, she had written a few funny things on the list to get it started—since her whole family loves chicken and dumplings, the first entry was, "If you want to be a Smith, you have to love chicken and dumplings." As the list grew, she started to include more earnest entries about values she felt her children should adopt, and the document soon became a living statement of how that family lives honorably in this world.

Remember, your children's input is important—unless they feel they have a role in the development of the final product, they may not be very inclined to adopt its principles. You may need to diplomatically remind them from time to time, though, that families are not democracies, and this is not a one person, one vote circumstance. Their input is valued, but when it comes to health and safety, you have veto power.

As A Parent, You Are Your Children's Most Powerful Role Model

James A. Baldwin said it best when he wrote, "Children have never been very good at listening to their elders, but they have never failed to imitate them." This is a really scary thought--you are always being watched! Your actions, both good and bad, will ultimately be mimicked by your children. Parents who smoke automatically ensure that their children are more likely to smoke also.[xxiii] On the other hand, Jonathan is a voracious reader, and our 6-year-old daughter is a reading maniac. The point is that everything we do is a message, a how-to manual for our children. If you dart in and out of the carpool lane without regard for the double yellow line, you may get to your destination a few minutes earlier, but you will also teach your children that rules can be broken if they are inconvenient or frustrating. If you drink *every time* you socialize, you teach your children that in order to have fun, you have to drink.

This does not mean you can't drink—it means you have to be aware of patterns. Occasional, moderate alcohol use that isn't immediately followed by driving is a relatively benign way for non-addicted adults to inject a little fun into a social situation, but if you always socialize by using alcohol it's possible your children will learn the lesson we talked about earlier, "I need alcohol to have fun and be social." If you drink, you don't need to stop in order to protect your children, but you should teach them moderation by behaving moderately. Remember, though, some things that can be done relatively safely by adults can't be done safely, even when done moderately, by children or teenagers. You are always being watched. This will either benefit your children or harm them; it's your choice. If your actions lack awareness, we suspect the outcome will be much less positive.

Discuss The Consequences Of Use Before It Occurs

If there is one aspect of drug discussions that elicits an almost universal agreement by drug educators and counselors, it is that the consequences for drug and alcohol use should be clearly outlined *before* the use occurs.[xxiv] This is not an attempt on your part to say, "I fully expect you will use, and here's what's going to happen when you do." This is much more an effort to say, "I hope and expect you will honor our family values and not use, but I understand you live in a world where some people do use. If you choose to be one of those people, here is what it will cost you." Please don't predispose your children to the use of drugs and alcohol by expecting that it *will* happen. Remember, not all kids do drugs.

Unfortunately, today's use statistics insist that some kids are going to use. No parent wants their child to use, and yet someone's child will. It may be yours. By discussing the consequences of use before it happens, you are accomplishing a number of goals:

1. You allow your child to factor in the cost of an action, in exactly the same way we discussed in the curfew section. Of course, you can't establish an

exact punishment for an act that has yet to occur, but you can create a menu to choose from. The typical punishment will entail the pain of loss—what your child values most will define the nature of the punishment. The general areas are pretty universal—cell phones, iPods, cars, drivers' licenses, social events, musical instruments, sports activities, freedom—anything a child values is on the table as a consequence of use.

As always, the punishment should fit the crime. If your child is a sober attendee of a party where drinking and drug use are taking place, that's one thing. That same child drunk or high at the party is another thing entirely. If your child was the host who provided the drugs and alcohol for the party, that's a whole different ballgame. Each instance calls for a different degree of consequence.

We're not going to explore the philosophy of punishment and its effectiveness here; rather we'll choose to accept as the norm that parents usually use punishment to motivate change in the face of undesirable or unsafe behaviors. Some people suggest, though, that punishment should not just be about taking away more and more of your kids' stuff until they acquiesce. We have heard the suggestion that punishment should be used to get children more involved with activities that will teach them a lesson about the nature of their behavior. Maybe children caught drinking or using drugs should spend some time doing volunteer work at a drug rehab where kids like them are trying to get clean and sober. Children caught drinking and driving might learn something valuable at a meeting where parents speak of the loss of their beloved child or spouse at the hands of a drunk driver; or they could spend a few weekends handing out literature at a DUI checkpoint. We're not advocating one form of punishment over another, just suggesting that punishment can take a lot of forms.

Finally, it should go without saying (that was a joke, by the way) that it is never appropriate to punish children physically or torture them emotionally in an effort to make them behave.

2. When you discuss the consequences of use with your children, you give them a *believable* way to deflect the offer of drugs or alcohol. One of the hardest things teens will ever do is say no to something other people are doing and not lose their friends. It's hard to maintain social status if someone is calling you a baby or a wimp. If your child can look another in the eye and say, "Really, I can't. If I get caught doing that my mom will saw my leg off with a butter knife," then maybe you have just averted a potential disaster. The declaration, "If I get caught I won't be able to get my license," has saved a lot of young people from using.

We want to make one really important note about negative consequences and punishment— make sure your stated consequences are not just empty threats. If you say you're going to do something, *you have to do it!* You will immediately lose most of your power and legitimacy if you impose a punishment and then let it slide after the first day. Many of our students know their parents are paper tigers. More than once we've heard kids say something like, "Yeah, they talk a lot, but they'll never stick with it." It's not just a matter of not living up to your word, either. When you threaten a punishment and then don't follow through, you are also making a statement that's loud and clear: "I don't really think this topic is as important as I said it is." Your kids will naturally reason that if it really mattered, you would have cared enough to follow up.

3. When you discuss the consequences of use with your children, you also open the door to discuss with them the consequences of *not using*. This allows you the opportunity to change behavior in a much more positive way, and we feel this is a much more proactive way to deal with the drug and alcohol issue in your family.

Teach Your Children To Set Goals, And When They Achieve Them, Celebrate!

We feel it's only fair that if you're going to punish use, you should reward non-use. One of the basic tenets of motivating people says you get better results by reinforcing desired behaviors than you do punishing undesired ones. One of Jonathan's old management trainers used to say, "You've got to catch them doing something right!" If you can arrange it so you can catch your child doing something right, you can reinforce that behavior by rewarding it. A lot of people create this circumstance by teaching their child to set goals. Start young if you can, start simply when you do, and base rewards on what your values tell you is appropriate.

A few things about goals: they should be clear, they should be written down, and they should have an end point—a point where success can be measured. Once a goal is met and rewarded, a new goal is set.

For years we've told the story of a mom and daughter who told us about their system. The goal was for the daughter to not drink or use drugs. The time frame was six months. The reward was two tickets to the concert of the daughter's choice—one ticket for her, one for a friend to go with her. Every six months, the mom and daughter would have an earnest discussion about whether the goal had been met. If it was determined that it had, the tickets were hers. If they ever determined that she had used, the daughter would have to go to school for an entire year without makeup. OK—going to school without makeup is not an earth-shattering consequence for most people, but to this young woman it was massive—this was something that really mattered to her! We knew this family for a number of years, and to the best of our knowledge, the daughter never did use.

Some parents have expressed concern about a system where a child's cooperation is up for sale. That's a valid point, but that's not what we're suggesting. The reward can take any form, some material, some more ethereal. Maybe the reward is a statement of your honest appreciation of your child's character, maybe it's a new right or privilege your child wants. Whatever form it takes, we think goal setting is a huge tool—we think you should use it.

Once The Goal Is Set, Help Your Child Succeed

When it comes to goals about resisting drug and alcohol use, Ronald Reagan's three words come to mind: "Trust, but verify." We are not making the declaration that your children aren't trustworthy; in fact, this isn't about trust--it's about health and safety. On the issue of trust, though, most parents would agree that teenagers, as a species, are relatively impulsive and unpredictable. It's not that they're untrustworthy as a measure of character, it's that even *they* don't know what they're about to do. The best laid plans will go out the door in a second if a socially powerful peer suggests something and everyone else immediately adopts that as the new plan. Here are a few things you can do to help your children meet their goals:

1. **Greet them when they come home from a night out.** You don't have to lurk in the front hall and scare them witless as they come in, but you should have a five minute conversation with your children immediately upon their return home from a night out socializing with their friends (or even if they were out on their own). Some moms recommend the "hug and sniff" greeting, and that's good as far as it goes, but just a few minutes of conversation is so powerful. First, it sets a baseline for normal behavior. If your son or daughter isn't usually drunk or high when they come home, but then one night they are, you'll probably hit on the change pretty fast. If your children know you'll be sitting there when they get home, they are *much* less likely to be completely polluted when they do. Greeting your children at the door isn't something that should begin when they are teenagers--start early and be consistent.

   As your children get older, their curfew may actually be after your bedtime. In that case, don't let them find you lolling in a puddle of your own drool at the kitchen table, and you can't really go to bed and expect they'll wake you when they get home. It's hard to tell the next morning if they really did forget or if there was a more nefarious reason for the lapse. Instead, here's the foolproof solution to the curfew vs. bedtime dilemma:

2. **_You_ sleep in _their_ bed.** When they get home, their first job is to wake you up and get you out of their bed. This simple effort ensures that you will get your 5 minutes of conversation, no matter how late their curfew is. If you have a teenage son, he may be kind of creeped out by the notion of you sleeping in his bed (not to mention how you feel about it!), and if that's the case, just do what one junior boy told his mom when she laid out the plan, "Bring a sleeping bag."

    The mother who taught us this said it started out as a police action, but ultimately it became the best parenting she ever did. As she described it, most of the time her daughter would wake her up and quickly report on the utter sameness of her evening out. On a few occasions each year, though, her daughter would glow with the excitement of something wonderful that had happened. But every once in a while her daughter would share with her something terrible that had happened—her heart had been broken, or she had witnessed something awful, and right when her daughter needed her the most, there she was. One of the most important roles a parent can play is that of a shoulder to cry on; but if you miss the immediacy of the moment, it will probably be lost. The feelings won't be dealt with by sharing them; by morning, they may just be buried.

3. **Call ahead.** When your children want to attend a party at another person's home, it really is your duty

to call ahead and find a few things out. These calls aren't required for 6-year-old birthday parties, but you might want to start the call-ahead pattern early so your children are trained to expect it when they reach their teens. The purpose of calling ahead is to find out the nature of the event. Most people will open the call with something like, "I understand your child is having a party, and I just wanted to know if there's anything I can do to help." If the response is, "Party?" you can be pretty sure this is a party you don't want your kid at—the parents of the host student aren't even aware the party is happening. If the answer is more along the lines of, "Thanks so much, but we're fine," at least you know the parents are aware of the party's existence. From about the 8th or 9th grade on, your calls should include a few more questions:

a. Will you be home for the entire evening?
b. Will adult supervision be present and adequate?
c. Will you be allowing alcohol or other drugs to be used or present? (Really, you do have to ask this.)
d. Will you be allowing young people to leave the party and then return? (Party safety 101 says once a young person is in, they can't leave unless they intend to leave for good.)
e. Will you call me if you have any concerns or problems with my child's behavior? (Wouldn't you rather know earlier rather than later if there are issues?)

If they haven't hung up on you or asked you heatedly what kind of person you think they are, and you are satisfied with their answers, you can be pretty sure your child will be safe at their party. If you've done your due diligence and you already know your kid's friend's parents, you won't have to make this kind of detailed call each time—just ring them up and ask the "Can I help" question and be done with it.

If the parent is unknown to you, though, you have to make the call. One thing that makes these calls so hard is that so few people actually do it. If more people called ahead, we'd all get more practice at making and receiving them gracefully when they are necessary. We've seen over the years that the norm is to not make the call. Parents regularly report to us that they've recently had a party at their home, and if 30 students and friends attend, usually only two or three parents will call ahead. If more parents called ahead, a lot of heartache could be instantly and easily avoided.

4. **Every once in a while, go into the parties your children are attending.** Yes, your children are going to die of embarrassment, but do it anyway. You might want to go in when you drop your children off (give them a 5 minute head start if you want to give them a break, but assure them you'll be looking for them immediately if things don't check out), but when they get older it will behoove you to occasionally drop in when the party is well underway. Lots of parents we meet hope, or naively assume, that drugs and alcohol aren't present at the parties their children attend. If they're right, great,

no problem; but if they're wrong, they really owe it to themselves to check it out.

5. **Have a code word.** The possibility exists that your children might find themselves in a bad spot. They may need your help getting out of it, but they just *can't* be seen calling mommy or daddy when things get hairy. If you have a pre-arranged code word that alerts you to your child's situation, you can arrange for their rescue without them having to directly ask you. A few things have to happen first for this to work:

   a. They have to start calling you on an arranged schedule when they are out with their friends. The younger you start this, the easier it will be to make it a habit. Every hour, every 90 minutes, every 2 hours; whatever you agree on, they have to call you at the appointed hour. You aren't just training *your* children here—you're training *their friends.* If their friends all know your kids have to make the call, they won't see anything unusual when the situation arises that prompts your children to use the code word.

   b. When they use the code word, *go get them.* Don't make them explain why they need you—that's why you have the code word!

   c. Plan and role play what it is that you'll say to get them out of there ASAP. Maybe you can say someone is sick and you need their help, maybe you can say their grandmother died again, maybe you just start yelling for no reason so your children can hold the phone up and complain, "Will you listen to this harpy? I gotta go, you guys." Whatever you agree is going to be said, it needs to be designed to get them out.

d. If your children are calling you because they're drunk or high, go get them—but don't use the "no questions asked" promise we hear about so often. Of course you're going to ask questions—it's your job! Everyone who works in this field agrees, though, that you don't discuss actions or consequences with children who are drunk or high. They won't remember what was said, it's highly unlikely you'll get any sense out of them anyway, and, most importantly, you're going to be angry and scared and emotional—now isn't the time to be making decisions or proclamations about what's going to happen. If you've already discussed the consequences of use with your children, you really don't need to talk to them about what's going to happen—that job is already done. Get them to bed, and deal with the rest in the morning.

We don't think you should spend a lot of energy worrying that your children won't call you if you insist on consequences for use. When you have the consequences talk, assure them as earnestly as possible that they are the most important thing in the world to you— you will *always* save them. Continue, though, that it is because you love them so much that you can't let something as devastating as drug and alcohol use pass without comment or consequence. (Maybe

48

you can bend a little, but don't do it until after the fact. If your children made a mistake, but after making the mistake they reached out for help, maybe the good judgment they showed by reaching out to you should be rewarded with a mitigation of the severity of the consequence. If they did the right thing in the end, it could make sense to ease up a little on the cost of their earlier poor judgment.) If you have agreed to a No Questions Asked policy, then you may have missed the opportunity to have a meaningful discussion about lessons that can be learned from big mistakes.

6. **<u>Do your children a favor—take their cell phones away when they go to bed.</u>** Here's one thing you can be pretty sure of—no good can come of a text message or a call on your child's cell phone after midnight. Just put the charger in your room, and each night the phone should find its way to the charger before your child goes to bed. Your kids are masters at networking, but they don't need to network at 1:00 a.m.

The 900 Pound Gorilla

There is one question that will *always* be asked if time constraints prevent us from covering it in the parent presentation—"What should I say if my kids ask me about my drug use?" Before we answer, let's go over a few basics. First, there is no universally accepted answer to this question. Some very smart, very accomplished people who work in our field disagree with our take on the issue. Second, lying is not an option, in our opinion. If you are going to lie when your kids hit you with hard questions, you're going to expend a huge amount of energy just keeping your story straight. If your kids do catch you in a lie, you're going to do untold damage to your relationship. By the way, lying won't work over time anyway. You might not realize it, but if you used to use drugs when you were younger, there are probably dozens of evidence bombs lurking in your attic and closets. We always tell parents, "If there's a picture of you in a tie-dyed t-shirt, wearing granny glasses, with The Who on stage in the background—you've smoked some dope! (If you're younger than us, insert the appropriate era's fashion and music, but the final point will be the same—you're caught!)

If you used to use drugs and want to lie to your kids about it, you have to burn all your high school yearbooks, burn all the love letters you kept, cease allowing high school and college friends to visit, and sever all ties to your family. Each of these will at some point or another put truth to your lie, and then it's game over. You have shown you are willing to manipulate your children with lies in order to make them do what you want them to do.

But if you're not going to lie, what should you do? Some people insist you should just not answer the question. We've heard speakers suggest that you should say, "This isn't about me—we're talking about you." Sorry, we think this non-answer is an answer just the same, but it's an answer without the opportunity for discussion. The non-answer advocates insist that a parent who admits drug use has in essence placed a bar which the child is now obligated to jump over. We think there's a problem, though—when a person refuses to answer, which way do you think the child will lean—toward a presumption of guilt, or one of innocence?

So you can't lie, and you can't refuse to answer, so that leaves just one option—answer. We believe that you *should* answer, but you have to answer exactly the right way. Here are some precautions you need to think about before you answer, though:

1. Don't answer if your children are not emotionally ready for the truth. If they're too young, just distract them. "Is that an EAGLE!?" usually works in our house.

2. Don't answer the question until it's *asked*.

3. If you're answering an older child's query, remember that the younger children will soon hear a replay unless you discuss this concern with the older child as a part of your answer.

4. Make sure you understand that, for this to work, you cannot currently be abusing legal drugs or using illegal drugs at all.

When you do answer, use this 3 step outline as a guide:

1. Your first sentence is, "Yes, I did." Notice the period at the end of that sentence. Don't go into graphic details about your drug use—no laundry lists of drugs you did, no party stories that might serve only to glorify your past use.

2. Your second effort should put your use into context. You are not trying to make excuses here; rather you're trying to explain the climate in which your use occurred. If you're Jonathan's peer, you didn't even *have* drug education in school—it just didn't exist back then. Also,

many of the drugs of abuse weren't even illegal back then. LSD wasn't illegal until 1966, ecstasy wasn't banned until 1985, and the date-rape drug GHB wasn't outlawed until 1997. Obviously, legal status doesn't make a drug safe or not safe, but legality goes a long way when explaining the context in which your drug use occurred. Here is one of the few times when pleading ignorance can be a positive—we really *didn't* know what we were doing! Another point to make here is that the nature of drugs has changed over the years—the dangers of drugs are better understood today, drugs are more widely available, and they are also purer and stronger than they used to be. This whole effort should not last more than a minute.

3. Your third point should sum up why you stopped. It isn't necessary to make things up, just think about how you came to your non-use position. Many people say they stopped because they just got bored, or that the promise drugs initially held had proved empty. Others say they stopped when they contemplated the idea of having children. It's really hard to be high *and* be a good parent; the two seem pretty exclusive. We kind of like how this last one sounds, too— "I stopped because I had you, and I only wanted to give you my best." If it's true, it's a pretty powerful thing to be able to say to your kids.

At the end of your answer, one of two things will probably happen—one, your children will be fine with what you've said and that will be the end of it, or two, your children will insist that since you got to learn through experience, they should have the same right and opportunity. If you find yourself confronted by an experiential learner, we think the best answer we've ever heard came from a letter written by a headmaster back east. The points expressed in the letter came to us via conversation, so we can't even give credit to the author, but their wisdom is too dear to pass up. In a letter to the parent body on the subject of experiential learners, which we'll paraphrase here, he said, "There are lots of things you don't have to take part in to know they are bad. You don't have to be a racist to know that racism is evil. You don't have to take part in genocide to know it's against the laws of God. You don't have to use drugs to know they are harmful--I'm here to tell you that." We think it's the best answer we've heard. It's earnest, it's honest, and it's to the point.

One last point about questions concerning your use—don't let your lack of prior drug use convince you that you can't adequately help your kids to not use. Parents constantly approach us with, "I never used drugs. I don't know how I can help my kids when it comes to drugs." This one kills us every time! We want to say, "Do you hear yourself? You never used! You're the perfect person to teach your child how to not use drugs! You're the role model!" It seems that, as a society, we are still stuck with the notion that the kids who drank and used and partied were the "cool" kids; that they were popular and the non-users were nerds. Seriously, it's time to get over it! First of all, geek *is* the new cool—you have now officially grown into being cool. Second, the popularity of users, and their prevalence, is overstated. There are actually fewer users than most kids imagine, and, if you really think about it, ALL of today's addicts and alcoholics came from the ranks of those who used—it's a requirement. It's time to stop thinking of yourself as a loser just because you didn't party in high school and college.

The other side of this last point is this—you are *not* a hypocrite if you used to use but you don't want your kids to. If you *still* use illegal drugs or abuse legal ones and you don't want your kids to, yes, you *are* a hypocrite. If, instead, you used to use, you stopped, and you now don't want your kids to use, you aren't a hypocrite, you're a *teacher*.

Watch Out For The Internet

This is not the forum for in-depth discussions on internet safety, but we want to go over a few cautions. We think internet connections represent a portal into a world of information that is unparalleled in our history, and yet because that information base is so vast it is both helpful and harmful at the same time. A child doing a keyword search on a drug term will be exposed to a massive array of drug information. Unfortunately, the majority of it will be about how to use the drug, how to get it, how to get around drug tests for it, how to manufacture it, and how anyone who says drugs are harmful is a liar or a puritan.

Please take the time to monitor your child's internet use. A lot of new information shows that kids are pretty good at steering clear of the most dangerous aspects of the internet, but we as parents need to maintain a watchful eye over what they see there.

Finally! The Last Two Things To Watch—
Your Medicine Chest And Your Liquor Cabinet

The Partnership for a Drug Free America says 1 of every 5 teens has abused prescription drugs.[xxv] The NIH says 20% of people in the US have used prescription drugs for non-medical reasons.[xxvi] The year 2006 was the first year where a child who decided to use drugs for the first time was more likely to abuse prescription drugs than they were to smoke marijuana.[xxvii] Prescription drugs like Vicodin, OxyContin, Valium, Ritalin and Adderall are growing in popularity every year, and it's time to wake up.[xxviii] Your medicine chest, if it contains any drug that might be abused, is a danger zone. Prescription drugs that can be abused don't belong in a place that is open and unsupervised. Drugs that can be abused belong under lock and key—that's the way the pharmacy treats them, why should our homes be any different?

Most parents wouldn't suspect that their children would be taking and abusing prescription drugs from home, but it really isn't just about your kids. What about the friends that visit (and this includes your friends); are you sure about all of them? It's like the old saw—strong locks keep people honest. You are the second or third most likely source of prescription medicines that are abused by teens.[xxix] You can help stop the flow of prescription drugs into your child's world by doing this very simple thing—take the drugs with the potential to be abused out of your medicine chest and secure them.

While we're on the subject, we should also note that over the counter (OTC) drugs are also potential sources of abuse. Most cold medications contain dextromethorphan (DXM) which can cause a high when taken in large doses. Stimulants like caffeine and ephedrine can be found in cold, sinus or diet pills. Even though these OTC drugs are legal and available, they can be dangerous or fatal when abused. Children who take cold medicine before bed when they have a cold are not what we're talking about here, but if you were to find two or three blister packs of Coricidin Cough and Cold (CCC or "skittles") empty in your trash can, you'd have a totally different, and dangerous, situation on your hands. It's time to get aware about the medicines we keep in our homes.

Also, if you have a bar in your home, or a liquor cabinet, you need to stay on top of your inventory. Teens report that their parents' liquor cabinets and bars are a huge source of alcohol they abuse. If you do drink in your home, you don't have to stop. You do, however, need to responsibly monitor how much you have in stock. If you had two cases of beer yesterday, but today you only have one, something happened—you had a party, you drank all of it yourself and therefore need to go to rehab, or somebody made off with some of your beer. You need to know where your alcohol is going.

Water and vodka look the same when they're in a vodka bottle. Occasionally, you need to make sure that your clear liquors—vodka, gin, rum, tequila, etc.—are still actually alcohol based liquids and not just water that has been cleverly substituted by your teen. Taste your clear liquors occasionally, just to be sure. Some parents have tried putting marks on their liquor bottles as a way to keep track of what they have. A restaurateur recently told us a trick about how to mark the amount of liquor in a bottle in a way that might not be so obvious to the casual observer. Instead of marking the bottle as you might normally (with the bottle standing upright), turn the bottle upside down, so the neck is facing downward, then mark the bottle, turn it back over and return it to your liquor cabinet. Many teens will see the mark, but few will figure out this simple system. Again, we do not consider all teens to be evil little trolls that steal and abuse drugs and alcohol. We do, however, hear more stories than we'd care to about teens that get into very dangerous situations that begin with drugs and alcohol obtained in the home.

One Final Thought

In the face of all this, it's sometimes hard to imagine how we can ever enjoy having kids in our lives, and yet that's what makes all this worth the trouble. Our daughter is the most amazing thing that has ever happened to us by a factor of 1000. When things get rough, as they are sure to when you love something that is human and flawed and tempestuous and driven by impulse, it pays to remember one thing—the way you felt when that little wonder first entered your life. Jonathan insists the whole world changed the day the nurse put our daughter in his arms for the first time—it was when he learned how to love.

No matter what form it took, remember what your dreams were on the day your child entered your life. What were your intentions that day? What dreams did you dream about what you and your child would become? When times are tough and life gets scary, remember those intentions—they are what give us the strength and the passion to carry on. For carry on we must—it's the job we signed up for. It's the most important job on earth.

Part 3

How did you two become the drug guys?

Kelly's Story: I am a drug addict magnet. I am the spouse, friend, family member and colleague of many alcoholics and drug addicts. Not just a few—a lot! My awareness of addiction began when I was in elementary school, but my understanding of it came when I was a teenager. Because I have so many people in my life who are in recovery, I must respect their anonymity. For that reason I will not be describing my life the way that a recovering alcoholic/addict would do in an autobiography, but I can tell you about how it affected me.

When I was 19, I decided to get my Ph.D. and work with friends and family members of addicts. After having several people in my life who were forever changed by their addiction, I realized that my life was changed by the experience as well. From my perspective, when they needed help, I was the one who cleaned up the mess. I was the one who picked people up when they fell down, held people's hair while they vomited, comforted them and listened to endless babble about their life problems. They all seem to find me eventually. I got to the point where I just wanted to hide.

After a couple of years of college psychology classes, I started realizing that I was a big part of the problem. Attending Al-Anon and Alateen meetings helped explain the impact that these people and their behaviors were having on my life. While I wasn't an addict myself, I was willing to try several drugs and unfortunately liked several of them. Alcohol was not for me, I had a very low tolerance for drinking. It made me sick and I hated that out of control, sleepy feeling.

But since drugs and alcohol were such a prevalent part of the culture in the 70's and 80's, it was easy to copy my friends' behaviors when they started using drugs. Since I had no drug education at all, what I view today as common sense non-use decisions were not so clear to me back then. As a sickly kid and only child, I craved attention from my peers. I am the perfect example of the naïve lamb heading for the slaughter. These are the kids I watch for today that I label the "followers."

Each person experiences drugs in their own way, and some drugs were more attractive to me than others. I have dyslexia and ADHD, but at that time I was still undiagnosed. I am so hyperactive (or "naturally caffeinated" as I tell my students) that I found myself attracted to prescription and over the counter drugs that would give me clarity and focus or help me sleep at night. I also regularly sought relief, via the use of prescription and OTC drugs, from the pain of a previous back injury. I was self medicating, but it wasn't until much later that I learned what that meant. Fortunately for me, I was the type of person who was able to say, "I don't like what this is doing to my life," and so I stopped before it got completely out of control. My common sense finally kicked in.

In the early 80's, I watched as more and more people around me destroyed themselves with drugs and alcohol, and by the time I was 22 years old I had witnessed several suicide attempts by people close to me. I got scared and decided to abstain from alcohol entirely, which I did for years. Finally, after a few years of school, I realized that I had no desire to spend the rest of my working life listening to people's problems as a psychologist.

At that point, I changed course and went to film/theater school and fell in love with comedy. I had always been a big fan of Bill Cosby and Bob Newhart, and I thought their jobs looked like a lot more fun than my original career track. I guess the joke was kind of on me when Newhart went on to do such brilliant comedy as a psychologist in "The Bob Newhart Show." I spent the next 10 years working in television, theater and comedy clubs. In the early 90's, I was rushing madly from film school at UCLA to the set of Full House at Sony Studios to the Groundlings on Melrose to the Laff Stop in Newport Beach.

I loved it, and met dozens of goal oriented, focused people who were following their passion, but it struck me as odd that a disproportionate number of the performers were smokers, alcoholics, and addicts. It seemed like most of the funniest performers were cast from the same mold—depressed, self-deprecating, observational comics with very real alcohol and drug habits. This is when my eyes were really opened about the level of depression and addiction that enveloped the performers. But it wasn't just the performers—the writers were self-loathing and frustrated that their talents were not being rewarded with fame and opportunity, while the aspiring directors and producers seemed convinced they had to play the party scene to make deals. I was constantly dealing with drunks and smokers; not just on the stage, but in the audience as well. I was annoyed and frustrated.

Then, in January of 1992, I lost my home, my pets and all of my belongings in a fire caused by a faulty extension cord. Haunted by loss and heartbreak, I decided to leave California and take a job at a comedy club in Harvard Square in Cambridge. After a year of being in the coldest place I'd ever been in my life, a friend of mine said that she knew a comic that I should meet, because she thought we would have a lot in common. I had just opened my own comedy club, and was attempting to do something really special with one person shows. My first response was "NO, I don't date the comics!" It was the cardinal rule that Cindy Stewart, my good friend and long time manager of another comedy club taught me—don't date the talent! My friend finally wore me down and convinced me I should give this guy a chance. When I first saw Jonathan, my immediate thought was that he was too tall for me (I'm 5'1" and he's 6'2"), but I spoke with him briefly. We eventually met again at an event at the Hard Rock Café in Boston, and I said, "Yes" to dinner.

On our 6 hour dinner date, we told each other our stories. I'm sure he was thinking that I had an enormous amount of baggage, and I certainly thought, "Well, this guy is totally screwed up!" As I listened to his story, though, I realized we had more in common than I originally thought. By the end of our date, I found myself hoping we would see each other again—we had a lot to talk about! Yes, we did go on another date, and we have now been talking for over 15 years; first as a couple, then as business partners, then husband and wife, and finally as parents.

After one year of dating, Jonathan left on tour with a non-profit speakers program talking to kids about drug addiction. I closed the club at the end of the comedy boom and went on tour with Jesus Christ Superstar. As we rolled past the interminable corn fields that bus tours must suffer, Carl Anderson (the original

Judas) told me daily that I should take what I knew and start my own lecture series with Jonathan. As the tour was ending, I approached Jonathan with the idea. In typical addict fashion, he was convinced it would never work, but as you can see, my wisdom prevailed!

Jonathan's Story: My mom and dad were classic examples of parents in the 50's and 60's—dedicated, hard working, and willing to sacrifice personal needs and wants so their kids would have everything possible. My dad was and is a pillar of virtue. I've never known him to lie, he believes in honor and country, and he's never once abused alcohol or drugs. For most of my early years, my mom was the best friend I had. My favorite times with her were when company was coming over, and I was my mom's helper in the kitchen. She really valued the contributions I was making so her party would be a success, and we enjoyed each other's company immensely. Over the years, she became a seriously gifted artist, she could make friends with just about anyone, and she was downright funny when she wanted to be. The saddest day I've ever had in my life was the day she died.

When we were young, our family went on vacation each year to this idyllic campground on the shores of Long Lake in Maine. On the way, we spent lots of time with extended family. We regularly saw cousins, aunts, uncles and grandparents. I think that out of 1,000 people, 999 of them would have come out of the experience happy, healthy, and well-adjusted. I didn't.

I don't remember the first few times our family had to move, but I do remember that we moved way too much because of my father's career as a high-ranking naval officer in the nuclear submarine service. I was always the new kid in class, friends were something you lost, and permanence was an illusion. My dad's service required that he be away for extended periods of time; he was home for three months and then gone for three months. This alternating absence went on for many years as we were growing up. While he was gone, my mom was left with the job of raising four sons and a daughter by herself.

As I said, my mom was funny, artistic and caring, but she was a victim of her time—a lot of military wives of the day did as they were told, kept their complaints to themselves, took diet pills to look good, took sleeping pills to counter the diet pills, and drank to deal with the pressure. In her later years, my mom's drinking became more of an issue. We didn't appreciate it at the time, but problems with alcohol had plagued her family for generations.

The first emotion I remember feeling was fear, and that was followed closely by loneliness. I was terrified to be left alone in a strange new setting, be it school or summer camp. My relationships were sick, my role models were inadequate, and my heart was broken. My dad was a tough disciplinarian; my older brother became a troubled bully of a kid. We, in turn, weren't kind to our younger brothers when it came to name calling and beatings.

In light of all this, my first drug experience seems a foregone conclusion. I was in third grade, the new kid in class, and desperate to be liked and accepted by the cool kids. The coolest kid in our third grade class was this guy named Clifford. Now, Clifford was that guy who had been left back a few times already, and he was much older than the rest of the class. He was bigger and tougher than any other third grade boy, and most of the fourth graders for that matter. One day after school, Clifford said to me, "We're going over to my house to smoke cigarettes—you want to come?" In about a second I did all the calculations. If I got caught, my parents would be livid and the punishment would be mighty. If I said, "No," I would be a baby in the eyes of the boys I was so desperate to impress. If I said, "Yes," the other boys in the class would know I was one of Clifford's smoking gang, and I would be granted the status associated with that position. To me, this was a no-brainer—I was going to smoke cigarettes in Clifford's garage.

My memories of my first cigarette are still clear—it was horrific. The smoke burned my throat, sinuses, and lungs. My eyes watered, I was so dizzy I thought I would fall down, and my stomach was doing flip-flops. My hands shook and I was pouring sweat. The taste in my mouth was so awful all I wanted to do was spit, but we were in Clifford's garage, so I just kept swallowing the nauseating saliva I was producing in such copious quantities. In all, it was the worst thing I had ever purposely done to myself, and yet in my eyes it was so worth it. I got to be a part of something I so desperately wanted—these guys acted like I was their friend. As a group, we mercilessly teased the one guy who changed his mind and wouldn't smoke. Finally, I wasn't the target of the barbs—I was the one delivering them. Smoking, as nasty as it was, made me a part of a peer group. Smoking socialized me when nothing in my almost nonexistent skill set did. Smoking fixed me.

Of course, I got caught, and I got punished. I don't remember the specific consequence, but it really didn't matter—what I got from smoking was so much more valuable to me than any price I had to pay. I felt guilty about the difficulty I caused my parents. Guilt was a constant co-morbid condition with the ever-present fear and loneliness, but at least I could push my feelings out of my head for a little while when I was with those guys and smoking like they were.

The next couple of drugs I used, alcohol and marijuana, followed pretty much the same pattern. I drank alcohol for the first time at the age of 12 in an effort to win the favor of a kid named Mike, and I smoked weed for the first time at 14 so my brother and his friends we were driving around with wouldn't tease me if I refused. The major difference with these two drugs versus cigarettes was their power to awaken euphoria—that drug high that is so powerful in its ability to erase those negative feelings for a while. Drunk to me wasn't stupor, it was exhilarating and liberating. I felt light and free and, for the first time in my life, I wasn't afraid of everyone around me. The idea of asking a girl to dance didn't inspire terror when I was drunk; in fact, it didn't scare me at all. Smoking weed was different from being drunk, but it was the same in that it made me not feel, and to me that was a relief in itself.

Author's note: None of this is an attempt to blame my addiction solely on outside forces, nor is it an effort to deflect responsibility for my choices, but I have a huge problem with the idea that addicts choose their path in the beginning or choose to remain addicted because they are weak or lack character. My early decisions to use took place when I was a little boy. I don't know if words can adequately convey the loneliness and emptiness that gripped me. I've heard hundreds of addicts describe this feeling--they have a huge, empty hole in their chest, and drugs fill that hole up. The notion that I had the ability to understand the consequences of my actions at that age is ridiculous.

The other common misconception about addiction I feel needs to be addressed here is the idea that an addict chooses on a daily basis to remain addicted. I encourage anyone struggling to understand how addicts work to first strive to understand the concept of the involuntary nature of denial and how it enslaves the addicted mind. I did not wake up each day and make a conscious choice to keep killing myself and breaking the hearts of those who loved me. The mind of an addict, in what has been described as an attempt to protect the ego, blinds itself to the day to day reality of the addiction. Yes, my use was my choice and mine alone. My addiction, however, once it took hold, lay largely beyond any real choice.

How, then, does anyone ever enter recovery? To me, recovery becomes possible when circumstances conspire to breach the wall of denial behind which the addict survives. Every once in a while, the blindness of denial will lift, and a small, fleeting window of opportunity will open. It doesn't usually stay open long, and, if the opportunity to see oneself clearly isn't quickly acted upon, it slams shut. With the power of perfect hindsight, I now see many windows of opportunity that I failed to capitalize on in my addiction, but that failure does not in any way represent a desire or choice on my part to remain an addict. At the time, I just didn't understand them or see them for what they were.

Drug use became the default setting for me when I socialized—if I was with friends, I was always trying to construct a setting in which drug use was possible. I chose friends who would use with me so my doubts about the rightness of using were less troubling. Even when I did find friends that wanted to use, almost none of them wanted to use the way I did. My desire for drugs was limitless—at the end of a binge, when everyone else just wanted to call it a day and crawl home, I just couldn't seem to turn it off. The only thing that ever stopped my use was money. Eventually, my cash would run out and my credit would dry up, and I'd have to temporarily stop simply because I had run out of options.

As a young adult, cocaine was my main drug of choice. No matter how much money I earned, it was never enough. A business I got involved with in the 80's provided a ready source of cash, and I bled it to the fullest. Of course, cocaine purchased by sloughing off inventory is a sure sign of impending business disaster, but just before the inevitable crash I got promoted into management. Today it might not make a lot of sense, but in the early to mid 80's there was enough cocaine being used by white collar druggies that even my use blended in. A lot of the people I worked with were flush with cash, and cocaine was pretty heavily present when we socialized. One prospective employee who interviewed and trained under me told me years later that he was convinced there was no way he was going to be hired by our company unless he started snorting coke—that's how rampant the use was at the time.

As I said earlier, though, my use always seemed more desperate in comparison. After awhile, I found myself much more interested in getting high than I was in anything else. I was doing a really terrible job at work. I constantly lied to my sales force about where I was and what I was doing. I either lied so I could dodge work and get high, or lied so I could dodge work and stay in bed for a few days trying to recover from a binge. When I was conscious enough to have feelings, I was wracked with guilt and self-loathing, and like any good addict, when those feelings bubbled to the surface I just nuked them out of existence with further, heavier drug use. Eventually, my bosses grew tired of my antics. I was called in and confronted—they didn't know exactly what was causing my shoddy performance, but they issued an ultimatum—fix it or you're fired. Totally incapable of telling the truth by then, I blamed my behavior on excessive stress caused by the job.

My bosses were really good people, and they offered me an out—go see the company psychologist and get some help. When I went to my first meeting with her, we hadn't been talking for more than 10 minutes when she put down her pen and said, "OK. That's enough." Confused, I asked her what she meant. She said, "Here's all you need to know. You're a drug addict and an alcoholic, and you're going to die if you don't check into treatment." When I tried to dodge and manipulate, she rephrased her initial comments with, "You're a dead man. You're just not smart enough to fall over yet."

For those of you who haven't spent a lot of time around addicts, she really wasn't as mean and heartless as she sounds—she just knew that the only way she could quickly break through my years of denial was to utterly shock me, and her words actually had their intended effect. For the first time in more than two decades, I had an honest conversation with someone about the real nature of my use. She agreed to help me, and set about finding me a place to go to drug rehab.

I was lucky enough to work for a company that at the time was willing to pay for a 28 day inpatient drug treatment, and I was doubly lucky to be admitted to McLean's Hospital in Belmont, MA, one of the best drug rehabs in the country. They taught me what I needed to know if I wanted to live. They took me to my first 12 step meeting. For the first time since I was 8, I wasn't doing drugs. It was truly amazing to not want to die every morning when I opened my eyes. It was incredible to not have every word that came out of my mouth be a lie. I no longer had to spend each morning wondering if I was going to puke my guts out in a fit of hangover induced nausea. And yet, for all the initial relief, there was a long, painful recovery effort ahead.

My initial attempt to get clean lasted for 3 years. By then, I had been clean long enough to start to wonder if I was *really* an addict. I thought that maybe, just maybe, I had been wrong. I tried to use again in a relapse that lasted a little more than 3 years. My hopes that maybe I wasn't really an addict were very well destroyed at the end of that phase of my use. I had and have a complete inability to use in a controlled fashion. At the time of this writing I have been clean for about 19 years. Hopefully, I won't have to relearn the truth of my addiction again—I certainly don't relish the idea of another stint in rehab.

I think it's important, before I end this section, to note how amazingly fortunate I am. There is a common refrain you'll hear if you spend time around addiction: that each addict will only decide to get help after reaching what is called a "bottom." A lot of people insist that addicts will only get help if they have been truly and utterly destroyed. I'm sure there's some truth to that notion—nobody checks into rehab because they have too many friends or because they're having too much fun. People go to rehab because things have simply gotten too ugly and, most importantly, the drugs have just stopped working. The point at which each addict decides they can't take any more can vary considerably. An addict that enters rehab early in the process is sometimes called a high-bottom addict; one that comes in with just one more breath left in their body is a low-bottom addict. Despite all the suffering I describe, I was a very high-bottom addict. When I got into rehab, I still had a job, I still had a house, my health was not completely destroyed, I hadn't killed anyone, I had no criminal record, and none of my drug associates wanted me dead. Granted, a lot of the material things were soon to be lost, but I was alive and I was free.

Maybe I'm just a wimp who couldn't take the heat that being a really accomplished drug addict exposes one to, but I'd rather credit my entry into treatment to something less negative—I'm just really lucky. I hear, on a daily basis, stories of heartbreak, destruction, despair and death caused by addiction. My mind boggles that anyone can survive, and often thrive, after going through what some addicts have. I am awed by their capacity to carry on, and I am thankful I didn't have to suffer the lesson at that level of intensity.

Then and now -- 19 years of recovery later: When I think about the differences between what I was like as a person when I was using addictively and what I am like now as a non-user in recovery, I am most likely to think about my relationships. Family relationships are the most powerful and influential, and family includes first the people you come from and then later the people you join with and create.

When I was using, the only relationship I had that mattered was the one I had with whatever drug I had gotten my hands on. I was willing to sacrifice any personal relationships I had in order to get the drug, and those meant families, friends, loved ones--all were considered expendable when it came to using. There are a thousand different reasons why it ended up this way, but suffice it to say for our purposes here that I felt terrible almost all the time, both about myself and my place in the world. The only time I didn't feel that way was when I was high, and I never wanted to feel that way, so I tried to stay high all the time.

Of course, if you know anything about drug use on this level you know that emotions can't be effectively fixed by using. Tolerance kicks in, money problems become omnipresent, good relationships turn bad and sick relationships become downright destructive. All this leads to feeling worse than ever, and if you're like I was and drug use is your only coping skill, it soon turns into an ever increasing spiral of use followed by feeling bad followed by more use and on and on and on.

The biggest difference between then and now is how I choose to act when I feel emotions. I'm probably never going to be the poster child for high EQ, but I have picked up a few of the basics. I know that I can't change anything but myself and how I feel about any given situation. I know that doing the right thing will not necessarily be rewarded by life immediately changing for the better. I know that being loved is more likely to happen to someone who has the capacity to love. I know that when I feel frustrated, angry outbursts and hurtful comments don't result in a reduction of that frustration but always make me feel guilty afterward. I know that feeling good is not the first step in the process, but the result of a continued striving to be good.

Most importantly, though, is the difference in how I treat my relationships today as opposed to when I was using. When I was using, I simply could not put anyone else first, ever. Granted, today I'm not necessarily that much better, but at least it is in my head that I should try. If someone else cooks, I should clean up. If something is important to my wife or daughter, then I should support that even if its value is not immediately apparent to me.

Finally, it also occurs to me that while I may have been born with certain potentials, that which I became was a person created in the crucible of environment. My emotional environment as a child and young man was an awful, hurtful place. I have the power, as a sober and recovering addict, to make sure that it doesn't happen again. My daughter will never suffer the abuse I did, and she will know every day that she is valued and loved--because I will tell her. Who she becomes is certainly not just in my hands, but to a large extent the environment in which she grows up is, and that is the biggest difference between me then and me now. Today, there is nothing more important to me than my wife and daughter, and that, amazingly, is a place I have found I can be happy.

Miles To Go Begins

Miles To Go started in earnest on Jonathan's 41st birthday. Kelly was growing weary of the lifestyle of the Broadway bus tour—put on the show, pack it up, drive all night, then wake up in yet another parking lot at another faceless venue. Jonathan was worn down by the demands of being a travelling drug educator--the constant air travel and the not-so-subtle dysfunctional dynamics of 22 recovering-addict educators trying to determine a pecking order. Kelly, always the visionary, had a plan. She was convinced we could take Jonathan's sense of humor, combine it with the story of his addiction and her role as caregiver and fixer of addicts, and with her knowledge of business and dramatic presentation create a better way to do drug education. We spent the next year developing a lecture series about addiction and drugs that was fun, scientific, and medically accurate while simultaneously retaining the power and emotion of our life stories.

We wanted our program to go beyond the slogan-based drug education so popular in that era. For too long, kids had been responding to drug education with rolling eyes and arms crossed over their chests— we wanted to educate, entertain, and engage them. Finally, in September of 1996, with the fundamentals of our program firmly in place, we moved back to California and started teaching. Our program became popular faster than we ever imagined, and we've been at it ever since. We are now, officially, "The drug guys."

Not All Kids Do Drugs
Lessons in Drug Prevention: Handbook One
Proactive Parenting techniques

To order any of our products or services, please visit:
www.milestogodrugeducation.com
Kelly Townsend, M.S. & Jonathan Scott
_____

[i] "Alcohol and Cancer, Alcohol Alert From NIAAA". About.com. 2010. August 22, 2010. http://alcoholism.about.com/cs/alerts/l/blnaa21.htm

[ii] Groch, Judith. "One Cannabis Joint Equals Smoking Up to Five Cigarettes". Medpage TODAY. July 31, 2007. August 22, 2010 http://www.medpagetoday.com/PrimaryCare/Smoking/6298.

[iii] "Youth Drinking Rates and Problems: A Comparison of European Countries and the United States". Join Together. 2005. August 23, 2010 http://www.jointogether.org/resources/youth-drinking-rates-and-a-of.html

[iv] "Drink Like the French, Die Like the French". Marin Institute. August 4, 2008. August 22, 2010 http://www.marininstitute.org/site/big-alcohol/15-industry-tactics/111-the-french-paradox-health-and-alcohol-use-in-france.html?start=8
[v] "Number of Alcoholics". eNotAlone. 2010. August 22, 2010 http://www.enotalone.com/article/5540.html

[vi] Guerrini, I. "Alcohol Consumption and Heavy Drinking: A Survey in Three Italian Villages". Alcohol and Alcoholism. February 14, 2006. August 23, 2010 http://alcalc.oxfordjournals.org/cgi/content/full/41/3/336

[vii] . "Children 'risking liver disease'". BBC NEWS. November 22, 2008. August 23, 2010 http://news.bbc.co.uk/2/hi/uk_news/7743265.stm

[viii] "Fact Sheets, Underage Drinking". CDC. July 20, 2010. August 23, 2010 http://www.cdc.gov/alcohol/fact-sheets/underage-drinking.htm

[ix] "Health Insurance and Substance Use Treatment Need". The NSDUH Report. July 11, 2008. August 23, 2010 http://www.oas.samhsa.gov/2k7/insurance/insurance.htm

[x] "Provide Treatment vs. Incarceration". Join Together. 2010. August 23, 2010 http://www.jointogether.org/keyissues/incarceration/treatment-vs-incarceration-readmore.html

[xi] Akens, Kirsten. "Sample Problems". Colorado Springs Independent. August 13, 2009. August 23, 2010 http://www.csindy.com/colorado/sample-problems/Content?oid=1404779

[xii] "Factors of Teen Drug Use". Adolescent Substance Abuse Knowledge Base. 2007. August 23, 2010 http://www.adolescent-substance-abuse.com/

[xiii] "Drug Abuse and Addiction". NIDA. July 28, 2010. August 23, 2010
http://drugabuse.gov/scienceofaddiction/addiction.html

[xiv] Emery, Chris. "Youthful Media Exposure Holds Promise and Peril".
Medpage TODAY. March 1, 2010. August 23, 2010
http://www.medpagetoday.com/Pediatrics/Parenting/18735

[xv] Dalton Ph.D., Madeline. "Relation between Parental Restrictions on
Movies and Adolescent Use of Tobacco and Alcohol". ACP American
College of Physicians. January/February 2002. August 23, 2010
http://www.acponline.org/clinical_information/journals_publications/ecp/ja
nfeb02/dalton.htm

[xvi] Ibid.

[xvii] "The Importance of Family Dinners V". The National Center on
Addiction and Substance Abuse at Columbia University (CASA).
September 23, 2009. August 23, 2010
http://www.casacolumbia.org/templates/PressReleases.aspx?articleid=567
&zoneid=66

[xviii] "Families, Friends, Schools and Neighborhoods Contribute to
Adolescent Alcohol Misuse". Science Daily. November 17, 2008. August
23, 2010
http://www.sciencedaily.com/releases/2008/11/081114080917.htm

[xix] Ibid.

[xx] "Parents Pivotal in Keeping Teens Away From Drugs, Reveals New
Data". PARENTS. THE ANTI-DRUG. February 9, 2006. August 23, 2010
http://www.theantidrug.com/news/press-release.aspx?id=19

[xxi] Ibid.

[xxii] "Drug Abuse and Addiction". NIDA. July 28, 2010. August 23, 2010
http://drugabuse.gov/scienceofaddiction/addiction.html

[xxiii] Gilman, SE, et al. "Parental smoking and adolescent smoking initiation:
and intergenerational perspective on tobacco control". PubMed.gov.
February, 2009. August 23, 2010
http://www.ncbi.nlm.nih.gov/pubmed/19171580

[xxiv] Cartwright, Ph.D., Kelly B. "Effective Behavior Management, Part IV". SelfhelpMagazine. July 7, 2000. August 23, 2010 http://www.selfhelpmagazine.com/article/bahavior-management-IV

[xxv] "Key Findings of the 2008 Partnership Attitude Tracking Study on Teen Drug Abuse". The Partnership for a Drug-Free America. May 1, 2009. August 23, 2010 http://www.drugfree.org/Portal/2008_Partnership_Attitude_Tracking_Study

[xxvi] "Prescription Drug Abuse". MedlinePlus. March 22, 2010. August 23, 2010 http://www.nlm.nih.gov/medlineplus/prescriptiondrugabuse.html

[xxvii] "Prescription Painkillers Becoming More Popular than Marijuana, SAMHSA Says". Join Together. October 30, 2006. August 23, 2010 http://www.jointogether.org/news/research/summaries/2006/prescription-painkillers.html

[xxviii] "Misuse of Prescription Drugs Common Among H.S. Students". Join Together. June 7, 2010. August 23, 2010 http://www.jointogether.org/news/research/summaries/2010/misuse-of-prescription-drugs.html

[xxix] "2009 Data from In-School Surveys of 8th-, 10th-, and 12th-Grade Students". Monitoring the Future. 2009. August 23, 2010 http://monitoringthefuture.org/